# I Like Weather!

# Why Is It Windy?

## Judith Williams

**Enslow Elementary**
an imprint of

**Enslow Publishers, Inc.**

| 40 Industrial Road | PO Box 38 |
| Box 398 | Aldershot |
| Berkeley Heights, NJ 07922 | Hants GU12 6BP |
| USA | UK |

http://www.enslow.com

# Words to Know

**anemometer** (ah neh MAH meh tur)— A tool that measures wind speed.

**Beaufort scale** (BOH furt SKAYL)—A way to show how hard the wind is blowing. The scale uses numbers from 0 to 12.

**hurricane** (HUR ih cayn)—A large storm that starts on the ocean and can move on to land.

**kilometer** (kih LAH meh tur)— A unit used to measure distance. It is shorter than a mile.

5-kilometer race

**tornado** (tor NAY doh)—A strong twisting wind that comes off a thunderstorm cloud and touches the ground.

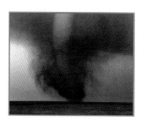

# Contents

# Can you see the wind?

No, but you can see when it is windy. The wind blows branches on trees. Flags wave on flagpoles. Dust blows in your eyes.

These are clues that the air is on the move.

5

# What is wind?

Air is everywhere. It moves from place to place. When it moves, we call it wind.

Two things make air move. One is the spinning of our planet. The other is the sun.

# What makes the wind blow all across the world?

Earth spins. This powerful spin pulls air with it. It makes the air go in circles around the Earth. This wind is grabbed by other winds across Earth.

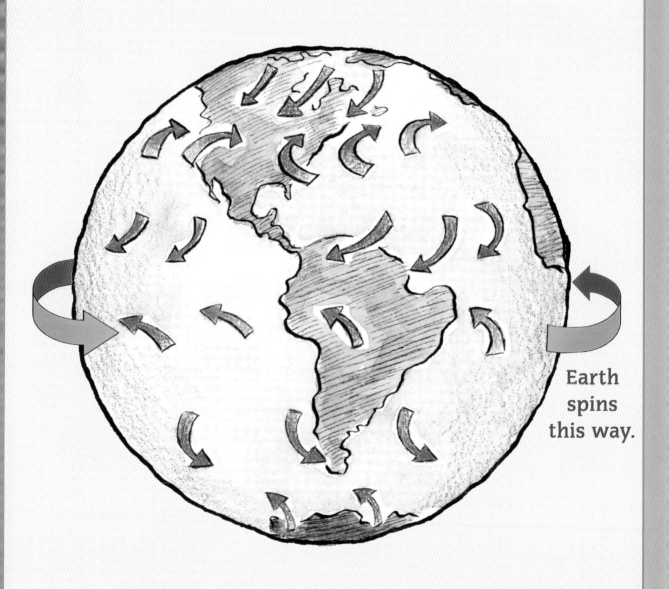

Earth
spins
this way.

The red arrows show how wind moves
all across the world.

# How does the sun make wind?

The sun heats the earth. Some places get warmer than others.

Air in the warm places rises into the sky. Cool air rushes in to take its place.

Air moving like this makes it windy.

Warm air rises because it is lighter than cold air.

# How fast is the wind blowing?

A special tool tells us how fast the wind is moving. We measure wind speed in miles per hour (or kilometers per hour).

A slow wind may go only 2 miles per hour, but a hurricane wind goes more than 74 miles per hour.

anemometer

A **tornado** can make winds that move faster than 300 miles per hour!

# What changes wind speed where you live?

Near oceans or large lakes, there is more wind. The water is almost flat. There is nothing for the wind to bump into to slow it down.

In cities, wind bumps into tall buildings. The buildings slow wind down a lot. Trees can slow wind too.

15

# How hard is the wind blowing?

The Beaufort scale gives numbers to show how hard the wind is blowing. The higher the number, the stronger the wind.

## The Beaufort Scale

| Beaufort number | | | Wind speed |
|---|---|---|---|
| **0** | Calm. Smoke goes straight up; can't feel wind on face |  | **0–1 mph\*** <br> 0–1.5 kph\*\* |
| **1** |  Light wind. Smoke drifts slowly with wind | | **1.1–3 mph** <br> 1.6–5 kph |
| **2** | Wind can be felt on face. Leaves rustle; flags and weather vanes move |  | **4–7 mph** <br> 6–11 kph |
| **3** |  Gentle breeze. Leaves and small twigs move; flags begin to extend outward | | **8–12 mph** <br> 12–19 kph |
| **4** | Moderate breeze. Dust and small papers blow about; small branches move; flags flap |  | **13–18 mph** <br> 20–29 kph |

\* mph — miles per hour    \*\* kph — kilometers per hour

| Beaufort number | | | Wind speed |
|---|---|---|---|

**5** — Fresh breeze. Small trees sway; flags ripple; whitecaps on lakes and ponds  **19–24 mph\***
30–38 kph\*\*

**6**  Strong breeze. Large branches move; flags beat; telephone wires whistle **25–31 mph**
39–50 kph

**7** — Strong wind. Whole trees move; flags extended; walking in wind is a bit difficult  **32–38 mph**
51–61 kph

**8**  Gale winds. Twigs break off trees; walking in wind is difficult **39–46 mph**
62–74 kph

**9** — Strong gale. Tiles or shingles may be torn off roofs  **47–54 mph**
75–86 kph

**10**  Storm winds. Small trees uprooted **55–63 mph**
87–100 kph

**11** — Violent storm winds. Lots of damage to houses and trees  **64–74 mph**
101–118 kph

**12**  Hurricane winds. Most houses and trees destroyed **>74 mph**
>118 kph

\* mph — miles per hour    \*\* kph — kilometers per hour

# How does the wind make you feel?

Wind can cool you off on a hot day. It can make you chilly on a cool day. Some days there is no wind, and other days the wind blows too hard for you to be outside.

But sometimes, a perfect wind can make a perfect day.

# How hard is the wind blowing this week?

You will need:

- ❖ the Beaufort scale drawing on pages 16–17
- ❖ 7 pieces of paper
- ❖ pencil and crayons

1.  On each piece of paper, write one day of the week.

2.  Draw a square near the top of the paper.

3.  Look outside on each day of the week. Look for things from the Beaufort scale to show you how hard the wind is blowing.

4.  Draw and color a picture to show what you see.

5.  Write the number in the square that matches your picture to the clues in the Beaufort scale.

How many days was the wind 6 or higher on the Beaufort scale?

# Learn More

## Books

**Bauer, Marion Dane**. *Wind*. New York: Aladdin, 2003.

**Cobb, Vicki**. *I Face the Wind*. New York: HarperCollins, 2003.

**Hewitt, Sally**. *Weather*. Brookfield, Conn.: Copper Beech Books, 1999.

**Williams, Judith**. *Searching for Stormy Weather with a Scientist*. Berkeley Heights, N.J.: Enslow Publishers, Inc., 2004.

## Web Sites

Federal Emergency Management Agency. *FEMA for Kids.* <http://www.fema.gov/kids/>

Miami Museum of Science. *Observing Weather.* © 2000. <http://www.miamisci.org/hurricane/wind.html>

National Weather Service. *Hurricane!* June 22, 2001. <http://www.crh.noaa.gov/mkx/owlie/hurri.htm>

# Index

Enslow Elementary, an imprint of Enslow Publishers, Inc.

Enslow Elementary® is a registered trademark of Enslow Publishers, Inc.

Copyright © 2005 by Enslow Publishers, Inc.

**Library of Congress Cataloging-in-Publication Data**

Williams, Judith (Judith A.)
  Why is it windy? / Judith Williams.
    p. cm. — (I like weather!)
  Includes bibliographical references and index.
  ISBN 0-7660-2320-6
  1. Winds—Juvenile literature. I. Title.
  QC931.4.W54 2005
  551.51'8—dc22
                    2004016791

Printed in the United States of America

10 9 8 7 6 5 4 3 2 1

**To Our Readers:** We have done our best to make sure all Internet Addresses in this book were active and appropriate when we went to press. However, the author and the publisher have no control over and assume no liability for the material available on those Internet sites or on other Web sites they may link to. Any comments or suggestions can be sent by e-mail to comments@enslow.com or to the address on the back cover.

**Photo Credits:** © 1998–2004 PictureQuest LLC, pp. 1, 18; © 2004 Dynamic Graphics, p. 14; © 2004 Fotosearch, LLC, p. 6; © 2004 Hemera Technologies Inc., p. 20; © 2004 JupiterImages Corporation, pp. 2 (hurricane), 4; © Allen Birnbach/Masterfile Corporation, p. 15; © Ariel Skelley/CORBIS, pp. 1, 19; © Copyright 1999–2004 Getty Images, Inc., p. 23; © Corel Corporation, pp. 8, 11; © Ken Lucas/Visuals Unlimited, p. 7; © Ken Davies/ Masterfile Corporation, pp. 1, 5; © Marc Epstein/ ... als Unlimited, pp. 1, 22; Michael Skrepnick, p. 21; © Sci... / Visuals Unlimited, pp. 2 (anemometer), 12; Reed T... ... m Bishop/Jim Reed Photography/Science Photo Lib... ... 2 (tornado), 13; Tom LaBaff, pp. 2 (Beaufort scale, ki... ... 9, 10, 16–17, 20.

**Cover Photo:** © 1998–2004 PictureQuest L...

Every effort has been made to locate ... ...right holders of material used in this book. If an... ... or omissions have occurred, corrections will be ... ... future editions of this book.

*Series Literacy Consultant*
Allan A. De Fina, Ph.D.
Past President of the
New Jersey Reading Association
Professor, Department of
Literacy Education
New Jersey City University

*...ience Consultant*
Harold Brooks, Ph.D.
NOAA/National Severe
Storms Laboratory
Norman, Oklahoma

*Note to Parents and Teachers:* The **I Like Weather!** series supports the National Science Education Standards for K–4 science. The Words to Know section introduces subject-specific vocabulary words, including pronunciation and definitions. Early readers may need help with these new words.